BRITISH

HUMAN

RIGHTS

FOR YOU

FOR ME

FOR US.

The UK Human Rights Act is a law that has protected each and every person in the UK since 1998.

It is the UK's foundation of Human Rights, to treat everyone Inclusively, Fairly, Equally and most important, with Dignity.

If anyone, in or with, power violates any of our rights, or fails to protect them, the Human Rights Act allows us to peacefully seek justice.

Articles 1 & 13

Articles 1 and 13 do not feature in the Act. This is because, by creating the Human Rights Act, the UK has fulfilled these rights.

For example, **Article 1** says that states must secure the rights of the Convention in their own jurisdiction.

The Human Rights Act is the main way of doing this for the UK.

This is established in the UN Universal Declaration of Human Rights and the European Convention on Human Rights.

Article 13 ensures that if a person or persons rights are violated, they are able to access effective support and justice.

This means they can take their case to a fair court to seek a judgment. The Human Rights Act is designed to ensure this happens.

What does the Human Rights Act do to protect us?

The Act has three main effects:

1. You can seek justice in a British court
It incorporates the rights set out in the European Convention on Human Rights (ECHR) into domestic British law. This means that if your human rights have been violated or called into question, you can take your case to a British court rather than having to seek justice from the European Court of Human Rights.

2. Public bodies must respect your rights

It requires all public bodies (like courts, police, local authorities, hospitals and publicly funded schools) and any other organisation carrying out any public functions to respect and protect your human rights.

3. New laws are compatible with Convention rights

In practice it means that Parliament will nearly always make sure that new laws are compatible with the rights set out in the European Convention on Human Rights (although ultimately Parliament is sovereign and can pass laws which are incompatible). The courts will also, where possible, interpret laws in a way which is compatible with Convention rights.

BREXIT...

So far UK Citizens as of January 2021 still can elevate Human Rights cases to the European Convention on Human rights, however this may change in the future. A future edition of this title will reflect this.

This is a testimony to how delicate our Human Rights are and how easily they can be removed, overrun and changed.

THE
ARTICLES

ARTICLE 2

The right to life

The Government is required by law to take steps to protect our lives.

Interpretation:

Police must keep the people safe from harm and all public services must work to keep us safe. If a person dies under suspicious circumstances or while in government (ie. The Police) care it must be investigated properly.

Working separately, Article 1 of the 13th Protocol make use of the death penalty illegal under UK Law.

ARTICLE 3

A person must not be subjected to torture nor suffer inhuman or degrading treatment.

Interpretation:

No one should be treated in an inhuman way, suffer a loss of dignity nor be tortured in anyway, not matter what the situation.

This is an absolute human right. A breach of this can never be justified. Should a person be subjected to torture of any kind the Government must investigate fully and properly.

ARTICLE 4

A person should never be a slave.

Interpretation:

We must never be treated as slaves or made to work against our will, ever.
It can never be legal to enslave someone for any length of time.

It also means we all have a duty to report suspected forced labour and other forms of modern slavery.
This means the Government have a responsibility to investigate fully.

ARTICAL 5

A person has the right to liberty.

Interpretation:

We all have the right to be free and not have our freedom threatened or taken away except in very specific circumstances which must be justified by a government as in line with law.

If our freedom is removed there must be robust, tested and legal safeguards in place to protect us and allow appeal.

ARTICLE 6

We all have a right
to a fair trial.

Interpretation:

We should always be treated as innocent until proven guilty. By both the government and others.

If accused of a crime, we have the right to hear the evidence against us in a fair court, in public and in a reasonable amount of time.

We all have the right to legal advice and a lawyer even if we cannot afford to pay for it. The state must pick up the costs to enable this.

ARTICLE 7

WE MUST NOT BE PUNISHED WITHOUT LAW

Interpretation:

We should not be held accountable for crimes before it became against the law. The government have a duty to ensure the people understand what new laws are passed and which actions are crimes, so we understand when we are at risk of breaking the law.

ARTICLE 8

The right to a private and family life.

Interpretation:

Privacy: No one should be able to observe or watch us secretly. No one should be able to read our private letters, emails or data, nor listen to our phone conversations. Unless there is a very good reason.

Family: Everyone has the right to enjoy a family life in the way we choose. This also means everyone has a right to have relationships. We must not be separated from our families, and if we are, we have the ability to communicate and stay in touch with family members.

ARTICLE 9

The freedom of thought, religion and belief.

Interpretation:

We all have the freedom to practice our own faiths, religion or belief without discrimination. We have the right to public and private worship, teaching, discussing or show our commitment to these beliefs how we choose.

We also have the right to have no faith, we should not be forced to join any religious institution or activity against our consent.

ARTICLE 10

We have the right to free speech.

Interpretation:

We have the right to speak, and freely hold our own opinions and hear the views of others.

We have this right even if our views are unpopular or could upset or offend others that hear or see them.

However, it is only acceptable to stop a person from speaking or limit the audience for their views if their views cause harm to others in anyway as this is unlawful.

ARTICLE 11

**The right to peaceful
protest.**

Interpretation:

We have the right to peaceful assembly, to come together with others to peacefully express our views.

This means we must be allowed to take part in <u>peaceful</u> protests, marches, and demonstrations.

We also have the right to establish, participate in, or become a member of a political party or trade union.

ARTICLE 12

We have the right to enter marriage with who we choose.

Interpretation:

We have the right to marry who we choose and create a family. Providing we are legally old enough.

National laws on marriage can impede this right, for instance, marriage between close relatives is illegal.

However any restrictions in this right must be reasonable and not interfere with other Equalities, Human Rights or other laws.

ARTICLE 14

NO ONE SHOULD SUFFER DISCRIMINATION.

Interpretation:

Everyone is born free and equal in rights and dignity. Each individual's rights are equal in law.

No person should be treated unfairly or differently. We should not have our rights denied due to age, gender identity, sex, race, faith or no-faith, nationality, statelessness, disability, race, sexual orientation, or anything else!

The Government have a responsibility to investigate discrimination.

THE
FIRST
PROTOCOL

We have the right to respect to our property.

The Government or any public body cannot cause harm, remove or tell us how to use our own property without a good reason.

We have a right to enjoy our own property unless it bothers others unreasonably or causes harm.

The right to education.

All Young People, under the age of 18 have a right to go to school and a right to education. The state must support and ensure it has everything within its power to enable a young person to have an education.

The means an education without discrimination and ensuring freedom of religion. This can be a public, home or private education as desired.

The right to vote.

We have the right to vote to appoint our own Government peacefully.

We have the right to vote by our own choice for who we choose.

We can stand for elections ourselves if we want to.

The Government must hold regular elections. These must be free and fair.

We have the right to be informed of the outcome of any public vote.

Additional UK law to protect us

The Equalities Act (2010)

Since 2010 The Equality Act has protected everyone in Britain from discrimination, harassment and victimisation.

The Equality Act protects people from discrimination by describing people under what is known as protected characteristics.

The Equality Act, recognises nine protected characteristics:

- age
- disability
- gender reassignment
- marriage and civil partnership
- pregnancy and maternity
- race
- religion or belief

- sex
- sexual orientation

Situations in which you are protected from discrimination are:

- when you are in a workplace
- when you use public services like healthcare, education, fire, police, courts, etc.
- when you use private businesses, charities, and other organisations that provide services and goods.
- when you use transport
- when you join a club or association.
- when you have contact with public bodies like your local council or government departments

Anywhere that Diversity, Equality and Inclusion meet the wider world the Equalities Act is there to protect you and your human rights from discrimination.

If you need help.

The following organisations are there to assist you and offer further support:

Citizens Advice Bureau

www.citizensadvice.org.uk

Amnesty

www.amnesty.org.uk

Liberty

www.libertyhumanrights.org.uk

Equality and Human Rights Commission

https://www.equalityhumanrights.com

THE GLOBAL GOALS

In 2015, all world leaders agreed to 17 Global Goals (known as the Sustainable Development Goals or SDGs). These goals have the power to create a better world by 2030, by ending poverty, fighting inequality and addressing the urgency of climate change. Guided by the goals, it is now up to all of us, governments, businesses, civil society and the general public to work together to build a better future for everyone.

This is the most inclusive way to preserve our planet, economy and human rights in the future. Find out more at: **www.globalgoals.org**

Other titles by Tony Malone

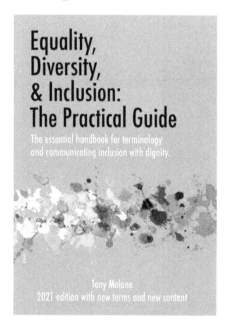

"The essential quick reference guide for EDI that should be on everyone's desk."

One of the best-selling books for Diversity and Inclusion in the world. This is an extensive glossary to terminology, a guide to faith diversity and a collection of thought-provoking articles on Privilege, Racism, Disability and more.

ISBN: 9798594986060

Published by:
Mendip Hills Studio Ltd
Printed using an environmentally considered process within the UK.

This edition: 1.1
Printed in January 2021 based on current rights.
This document is not intended to replace or assist with legal advice
rather give you a starting point to understand the complexities of
Human Rights as a subject.

A proportion of profit from the sale of this title is donated equally to
Amnesty International and Liberty UK

Tony Malone is an artist and Human Rights Activist. They have spent
over 20 years assisting rights causes across the world and continues to
do so. You can find out more on their website: **tonymalone.co.uk**

Printed in Great Britain
by Amazon